TURN NOW THE TIDE

JOE NEAL

Copyright © 2014 Joe Neal

All rights reserved. No part of this publication may be reproduced or transmitted in any form or by any means, electronic or mechanical including photocopying, recording or any information storage or retrieval system, without prior permission in writing from the publishers.

The right of Joe Neal to be identified as the author of this work has been asserted by him in accordance with the Copyright, Designs and Patents Act 1988

First published in the United Kingdom in 2014 by
The Choir Press

ISBN 978-1-909300-73-6

Edited by Harriet Evans
Portrait of the author by Tommy Clancy
Typeset in 11pt Cambria

ABOUT THE AUTHOR

Joe Neal was born half-way up a mountain in North Wales. He began his acting career in repertory theatre before attending Nottingham University. To supplement his income, he also trained as a journalist, working for the Western Mail (Cardiff), Times, Guardian, Daily Telegraph and Daily Express.

As an actor, he has performed on stage, radio and television in Britain and Ireland. Between acting work Neal writes extensively on the countryside and natural history as well as devoting time to poetry and short stories which he believes should be read aloud – 'even to oneself.'

A glutton for punishing experiences, he stood twice as an Independent for Parliament in Britain and once in Ireland for the European elections.

His published work has appeared in the Times, Daily Telegraph, Countryman, Waterlog, New Writer, New Society (now defunct), Ireland's Own, Scaldy Detail and numerous poetry magazines. Performed writing includes *Revenge*, *The Reluctant Trombonist*, *Send in the Clown* and *Kites and Catullus*. He has read the poems of Seamus Heaney and John Betjeman on BBC television and Shakespeare and Dylan Thomas on BBC radio. Recently he had 12 of his poems published in the anthology *Dust Motes Dancing in the Sunbeams*.

Turn Now the Tide is Neal's second collection of poetry and follows last year's publication of the widely acclaimed *Telling It at a Slant*. Both are available as readings by the author.

Neal says his life has been shaped by his childhood in North Wales and the Roman town of Colchester, Essex, and – more importantly – by time spent in Ireland, where he now lives. He is divorced and now a proud grandparent.

*T'ain't what you do, it's
the way that you do it.*

Trummy Young

CONTENTS

Foreword ... ix

BLANK CANVAS

Barbican Buffalo ... 1
Blowing in the Wind ... 2
Postcard Scene, 1910 ... 3
Love at First Bite ... 4
Out of Place ... 5
Rust Never Sleeps ... 6
Baby Blues ... 8
Com Soc Comrade ... 10
Baddie Two-Socks ... 12
Jump the Rabbit ... 14
Diplomacy ... 15
Please, Not Love Again! ... 16
Only Women Pop ... 18
Last Spy Standing ... 19
Worshipping the Word ... 20
Castle Oak ... 22
Balloon Buffoon ... 23
Ring Around the Radio ... 24
Sundays ... 26
Walking on the Wind ... 28
Blank Canvas ... 29
Turned On ... 32
Budding Schopenhauer ... 34

TIGER ON THE DOORSTEP

Shades of You	37
Off Beat	38
Never Ask	39
The Iceni Way, 1955	40
Come Back, Catullus	42
Down Basin Street	44
Rubbler Rhys	46
Shadows on a Wall	49
Getting On	50
Hot Gossip	51
Whisperer	52
Hiraeth	53
Curtain Call	54
Watchers	55
Cave Paintings	56
Rhythm of a Dive	57
Cold War Gran	58
In the Biblical Sense	59
Parrot Vote	60
Pike	62
Pathfinder	63
Not Quite Legless	64
Ye Shall Not Laugh	65
Ever and Ever	66
Tiger on the Doorstep	67
Another Bridget	68
Odd Izzie, 2001	70
Skyfall	71

RIVER SONG

Music of Antrim	75
Get Out of My Garden	76
Sky Walker	77
Into the Gulley	78
Ear Trumpet	80
Too Wet to Woo	81
His Fairy Queene	82
Alpha and Omega	83
Foxglove Fish	84
Turn Now the Tide	85
Catcher in the Sky	86
Riding High	87
Tumbling Down	88
Vinegar Hill	90
Begging Now	92
Mussel Man	94
Duck Call	95
Single-Handed	96
Mister Softee	97
River Song	98
Casting	99
Learning Curve	100
Love's Velocity	102
Guardians of Time	103
Prickle	104
What Shall It Be?	105
Day of the Dinosaur	106
Understanding Godot	107

FOREWORD

Joe Neal is a manipulator of words. His poems are a mode of transport for his ideas. His repository of experiences and images is his own business, but his poetry, full of magic properties when combined with his identifiable style and music, undoubtedly belongs to the world. He makes each word count double and as a consequence all the five senses are called into play.

Revisiting again individual poems in *Turn Now the Tide*, 'Barbican Buffalo' (*'All the trains I've caught since then bring that moment shunting back'*), 'Love at First Bite' (*'the promise in your smile is of something more to come'*), 'Shades of You' (*'You see, when I paint or draw, we're all the one, a passion marled and intricate, born on my palette'*), 'In the Biblical Sense' (*'but disquiet came in dreams of threesome romps'*) and 'Too Wet to Woo' (*'We shared a great hope when we met in the rain'*), I encounter not alone a man of letters who is unhesitatingly committed to the ideal of love, but an acute and sympathetic observer of the human condition.

From the outset, I received *Turn Now the Tide*, Joe's second collection, as a paean to beauty, to humanity, to music; what the poems share, filtered through the aperture of this poet's vision, though more susceptible to gravity than Wordsworth's 'inward eye', is an impeccable rhythm.

Though I have long admired Joe's fishing poems in the journal *Waterlog*, alongside notable contributions from George Melly and Ted Hughes, he is not exclusively a poet of the natural world. He is cosmopolitan and cultured, a legacy of his time as a journalist in London, rubbing shoulders with some of the greatest scribes of his age and indulging his love of jazz in Soho, before crossing the Irish Sea and retiring to Castlebridge, to be rejuvenated as an actor and as a poet.

I have seen Joe on stage dozens of times, from *A Child's Christmas in Wales* in Wexford Arts Centre and a Wexford Festival Opera production of *The Threepenny Opera* to an intimate but salubrious reading from *Telling It at a Slant* in Enniscorthy Castle, when he enchanted with more of a performance than a reading. Joe Neal doesn't abandon his poems when the print is dry; he cares for them lovingly, as they are the repository of cherished memories, a record of exchanges and experiences from another time and another place. Saying he is often haunted by voices would not be wide of the mark.

Joe's retreat from journalism in the media capital of the world to the idyllic haven of Eden Vale, where the trout in the River Sow ferry moonbeams on their back, was the actor and writer exchanging one stage for another. He needed space. He needed the clock of nature. He needed, ironically for one so sociable and equable, a form of solitude. His poetic vision – coiled in dormancy – required an oblique slant on his interests, yet he continues to sate what stirs his senses; admire his play with words in this e-mail to me while I was in London.

Dear Tom,

I envy you that evening of Wynton Marsalis; did he use his blocky-square-modular trumpet to blow golden bubbles from his lips? Or the more traditional horn, that makes and breaks its own mould?

And was it an audience of striking-looking punters who wanted to be seen? (The Barbican is like that these days.) Or were they Ronnie Scott's nodding people of the darkness? I used to be one of the latter, by the way, and still have my out-of-date membership card. These things are the stuff of poetry – as is Wynton when he runs free within his own prison of perfection. Marsalis nuda veritas est.

Bestest – Joe

Returning to the poems, 'Please, Not Love Again!' unfurls with the following stanza:

Oh, my Beatrice, I am
so hopelessly perplexed
by your wantonness
of beauty which teeters
constantly on the cusp
of ugliness when I forget
to say your name
the Italian way.

It is entirely in character for Joe the poet, with the DNA of Joe the classically trained actor, to appropriate one of the great literary muses of Western civilisation, and toy with the raw quintessence of beauty which so beguiled Dante.

'I grind those peppers of desire with the pestle of my being!' Joe's Beatrice, unlike Dante's, is not merely the optimistic figment of a colourful and inventive imagination. The poet is drawn to what he intrinsically understands, empirically and sensually. When he is not being aesthetically ascetic in his cottage in the sumptuously sylvan Eden Vale, Joe is a kind-hearted and kindred spirit of the arts in Wexford and further afield where, one will observe, he exudes a demonstrable empathy for the opposite sex. 'Empathy' is perhaps too weak a word. It lacks a pulse. It lacks the alchemy which is the livery beneath the spoken word of the poet.

To be on intimate terms with Joe's poetry is to know that he has the potential to see a Beatrice Portinari in most women, not necessarily as the incarnation of beatific love as painted by another Dante (Gabriel Rossetti), but as a depthless source of inspiration. In truth, Joe is closer to the Roman Catullus than the Florentine Dante, epitomising the former's skill in exploring the steps in a relationship and, as the raison d'être of the poet, the reluctance to relinquish the electricity of the experience, no matter how brief.

> *I still have her likeness, decades on,*
> *my Com Soc comrade*
> *– but not in arms.*
> *Oh, no.*
> *Free love? Alas,*
> *she never toed the party line...*

(from 'Com Soc Comrade')

There is a connection between his declamatory prowess and his choice of words, an unstated fidelity, as far as I know, to the belief that no poem that is not better heard than read is a good poem. His compatriot Dylan Thomas, whose centenary is later this year, and whom Joe remembers in 'Worshipping the Word' (*'With tribrachic stutter of his poem gun, he gave it to them – all five barrels of iambic pentagram'* – Thomas's invocation to the actors before the first performance of *Under Milk Wood* in New York), was a master of sound, sense and sensibility.

I have heard Joe deliver his poems with spellbinding diction on many occasions, including 'Tumbling Down' in this collection, which caught my attention because I hear the writer perform it when I revisit it, particularly the second verse.

Springtime's best when acrobatic
lambs flounce around the roof
and daffodils stand in
for the yellow of the morning sun.

The rhythmical phrasing is so acute: the phrasing dances, the joie de vivre is painted vividly. 'Tumbling Down' and these lines from 'Getting On', where the poet wonders whether he will be dragged away in the future

to join old ladies
playing Bezique
and drinking tea
with woollen rugs
across the knee

serve as a reminder that poetry is either suggestive or selective, with a dynamic as instantaneous as a shooting star, and a shelf life as short. Joe handles his subject with kid gloves, sensitively and without malice, with a deftness of touch as sure and as true as a fly-fisherman unhooking his quarry. He is, I think you will find, an honest poet, a fair poet, a writer who imbues his work with a quality which defines him: what Ted Hughes referred to as a 'healing benevolence'.

> *Until the night I saw,*
> *lighting up my doorstep,*
> *the incandescent colours*
> *of a garden tiger moth –*
> *reminder that your beauty*
> *had never left this earth.*

> (from 'Tiger on the Doorstep')

Though poets are reluctant to admit as much, the engagement between the poem and the reader has everything to do with the stab of recognition, that lightning ability to arouse, how a string of words segued by rhythm enters through the trapdoor of our imagination and engages the fearlessly protective memory.

Turn Now the Tide, to Joe Neal's friends and to those who know him through his poems, is an affirmation of a generous spirit, a writer unafraid to be true to himself, a writer for whom the aura of connotation cannot be at the expense of finding the right word, and for whom the distance between the literary and the familiar should not be an unbridgeable chasm.

But soon, with dawn, the time will come
when tide begins to draw away and the swoosh
and gush of unimpeded downstream
flow will bring again the music
that I have learned to see and know.

(from *River Song*)

Tom Mooney

July 2014

BLANK CANVAS

Blank Canvas

BARBICAN BUFFALO

Do you remember when,
after a first-night party,
we tapped and danced
the Buffalo along the Tube
platform and bellowed out
our finale song?

And how, at the Barbican,
a station man called Singh
had looked on, startled,
in his smart white turban
while we echoed down
the tunnel – step, step,
tappety step – and imagined
the crowd's applause?

Your forward journey took
you on to New York's
Broadway, mine to West
End theatreland;
but what of Mr Singh?
Does he dream of Bollywood
and dancers on the Circle Line?

All the trains I've caught
since then bring
that moment shunting back;
is it the same for you?

Turn Now the Tide

BLOWING IN THE WIND

On a scale of one to seven
I'm on the slide
– bit like my trombone;
ensemble playing's fine,
tailgate too (you growler)
but solo? – oh no,
you're not quite good enough
to blow the dust;
you're just for show.

It was different once;
while vinyl turned
at thirty-three and a third,
I gigged with music's best
– but no one heard.
They're all dead now,
they were all dead then.

Armstrong, Bechet, Jelly Roll
and Fats – and Kid Ory for duets,
and, in my later phase,
Mingus, Miles and John Coltrane,
but their sounds live on
– jazz that says it all
in notes of black and white
              – and blue.

POSTCARD SCENE, 1910

Down the pebbled beach
they trundled, horsedrawn
huts splashed by breaking
waves; and, oh, the shame!
Inside, on wooden seats,
sat laughing, seaside ladies
in their bain – frilly,
one-piece, skirted swimming
suits – out of sight
of men, for that was the way
in the summer of 1910 –
when a bathing machine
broke through time
from a postcard scene.

Turn Now the Tide

LOVE AT FIRST BITE

You are sitting at the sushi bar
watching food rotate;
your choice, I note, without debate
is chicken udon served with spice,
mine's a dish of that gyoza duck;

I offer you a wedge of it
and you respond with pepper
seasoned squid; no names,
no introductions – just the chewy
contemplation of Japanese cuisine;

We follow up with yakisoba
prawn, then plump for plates
of puffy pumpkin korroke;

Our tastes have intertwined
– this is now a dinner date
and the promise in your smile
is of something more to come!

Blank Canvas

OUT OF PLACE

I met you on the train;
serene you sat, in sacred
isolation from our haughty
heathen world – and yet,
still, we connected for a chat.

You said that you'd been born
in London and had never
seen your parents' home,
but had heard it was so beautiful
– so different from our boxed-in place.

And when I told you
of my North Wales
mountain habitat,
your bounded face lit up.

Exchanging views, I asked you
what would be the universal prayer
of your own people in Eritrea,
and you said: 'To seek a better space.'

But you could not hide
the tears that welled behind
your black hijab-begirted eyes.

Turn Now the Tide

RUST NEVER SLEEPS

I was a watchman once
– but not the kind that sat
beside a roadside hole
and fed a brazier with coal;

No, I was employed to repel
all boarders from a scrap-bound
tanker ship used by Customs
men to hoard their bonded goods;

Of thief there was no sign
but the nightmare noise
that put the fear of God
in me was the pit-a-pat
of rust-peeled paint that fell
continuously in broken time;

My companions in the ghostly
crew were Schopenhauer
and landlocked Kant
whose learned thoughts, my tutor
said, I needed in my head;

For exercise I ran the stinking
decks while gulls from a parallel
reality cackled in the sky
and added to the smears beneath my feet;

Some nights when I was bored

Blank Canvas

with philosophy I'd lean across
the anchored bow and signal flash
with my pocket torch at passing ships;

With the little Morse I knew I'd dot
and dash: HEAVE TO OR WE WILL FIRE
ON YOU – but they just steamed on
as if I did not exist at all;

From *The World as Will* I got my fill
– though if the pirate men had come
what could a pile of books have done?

Turn Now the Tide

BABY BLUES

'Please release me...'
Humperdinck in song,
workmen's wireless blaring
for all Maternity.

Up the steps and down
spotless corridors I wend,
heavy with the burden
of responsibility.

'...let me go...'
Too young to be a dad
with so many
hope-scattered oats unsown.

Then the scene before me:
she in bed and babe in arms,
wrinkled face, all red,
peeking from the fresh-bought
swaddling clothes.

And out they come,
those blurted words
so crushingly delivered:
'Oh, isn't he ugly?'

But you grew to be
our handsome prince
who inherited the world

Blank Canvas

– and, more importantly,
I met the greatest
friend I ever had.

Turn Now the Tide

COM SOC COMRADE

I join Com Soc at university;
I am a fresher, you see,
just starting my degree.

They say there are a lot
of women members
and free love's a political necessity.
Also, I get to be called comrade – which is cool.

So there's this girl called Vanessa,
comrade Vanessa, and all I want
is to possess her.

After our meeting at The Bell,
and several pints to break the spell,
she follows me back to my student cell
– my bed-sit – for a bit more dialectic.

And promptly falls asleep instead
(too much beer and Hegel in her head
– mine too, if truth be told;
thesis and antithesis,
but no synthesis to behold).

So what to do? I know, I'll sketch her,
a memento on the back of Marx's *Manifesto*.
One continuous, twirling line
– a technique learned in Art Soc –
pen never lifted until Vanessa is complete.

Blank Canvas

I still have her likeness, decades on,
my Com Soc comrade
– but not in arms.
Oh, no.
Free love? Alas,
she never toed the party line…

Turn Now the Tide

BADDIE TWO-SOCKS

As a child I think I loved my dad
– sometimes, when he laughed with me;
but mostly, it seemed, I made him mad
and he cuffed me round the head
or thrashed me for what I did or said.

At school it was just the same
if I didn't play the game;
strictly speaking, I was to blame
for I broke the rules deliberately,
hating ways they spoke to me
like I was just a simple tree
to bend their way.

So I wore my father's gaudy socks
– unmatched, just to vex –
and regiments of forbidden
badges on my blazer top;
Rockfist Rogan Fan Club made
me feel immune, and the Boys' Magic
Circle helped me vanish in a world
of make-believe – joining the *Eagle*
comic hero Dan Dare, spaceman,
in his fight to beat the evil Mekon.

Against all this, for good work
I gained more points than anyone;
but bad behaviour lost them

Blank Canvas

all again. It was my right, you see.
To cap it all, I learned to box
– to protect myself and beat
the playground bully thugs.

But what to me was greatest fun
was when I mimicked staff
and found warmth of laughter
with the other boys and girls.
He's out of our control, the reports
all said; and then I knew I'd won.

Turn Now the Tide

JUMP THE RABBIT

Hear the shimmer, see the sound,
laughter chastens sadness
in the rhythm of the round.

Hop the crotchet
– coruscate!

Jump the rabbit
– syncopate!

Life's the beat of jazz
– improvise!

Ragtime sees you right
when you conjure colour
out of black and white.

There is Here. Then is Now.
Don't you feel it?
                      Wow!

DIPLOMACY

The twist
of the word
when you
squirt
it with oil
will turn
on the truth
and poison
the soil
of nations
with blood
that's ordered
be spilled
on behalf
of the men
who trumped up
the lie

PLEASE, NOT LOVE AGAIN!

Oh, my Beatrice, I am
so hopelessly perplexed
by your wantonness
of beauty which teeters
constantly on the cusp
of ugliness when I forget
to say your name
the Italian way.

How you taunt me,
you the mortar
of unattainability,
as I grind
those peppers of desire
with the pestle of my being!

You are the Clodia
to my Catullus,
teaser of the teased,
and ever out of reach.
Is that what love
is all about?
Must I wonder yet again?

But I'll reiterate
(and maybe win
a smile from you):

Blank Canvas

Beatrice, I love the way
you say your name
the Italian way!

Turn Now the Tide

ONLY WOMEN POP

A busy, bustling woman
pops down to the shop.
But me? Well, I never pop;
it's just not done
– like the buttoned-up
pyjama top.
No, popping's
for the fairer sex;
men wander, nonchalantly,
and may take in a pub
along the way.
Or not.
It all depends…

Blank Canvas

LAST SPY STANDING

I am the Thirteenth Man,
but I must confess
I'm not a superstitious spy;
the eight you didn't know
about were simply everywhere.

It was your belief in other
people's innate goodness
that kept us hidden in the box;
all this political correctness,
that's what made the secret stick.

But now this traitor has been
outed by his mortality;
to find the name, Moscow rules
apply – the chalk mark means
you look beneath the ladder.
                              Bad luck.

Turn Now the Tide

WORSHIPPING THE WORD

With tribrachic stutter
of his poem gun,
he gave it to them
– all five barrels
of iambic pentagram.

Worship the word,
each stanza said,
romance is so passé
– dead dead dead,
gone away.

And when he'd finished
gutting the Divine,
he turned his sharpened
tongue to Nature
and the Corydon
– to nostalgia
and the pastoral theme,
while ghosts of Wordsworth,
Byron, Keats and Shelley
shuddered in their
serried ranks
of nodding daffodils.

Howdy, we called him,
the nihilist in a cowboy hat
– peripatetic poet

Blank Canvas

who hawked his hate
in barrow-loads of pap.

Still, he had a point
about our high-tech
lemming dash to the abyss
of pornographic nothingness.

CASTLE OAK

I was that tousled boy
who tugged and shook
the little tree
atop the Roman tower
– who should have been
expelled, not just
from school, but from
the whole of society.

But the castle oak
lived on, too strong
for a child bored
with history;
and still it stands,
tall and straight –
unlike the man,
now hairless,
who wanted to thwart
the march of time.

Blank Canvas

BALLOON BUFFOON

Pear-shaped shadow
passes over pasture,
making frightened cows stampede
– no milk tonight, the farmer
rages, but plenty drink above
as toffs in drifting basket
toast their red balloon.

Empty champagne bottles
come dropping from the sky
to be collected by the chauffeur
as he follows in the Rolls,
his job to pay for greenhouse
damage by his master riding high.

Based on a Times news report, 1908

RING AROUND THE RADIO

Linked by quiet delight,
they savoured Nellie Melba
as she sang to them –
Gran, her mum and dad,
sitting in the scullery
earthed to a water pipe
and wired to the washing line.

The concert brought to them
Ella Shields doing her
Burlington Bertie bit –
and Clarice Mayne's
infectious Joshuah
– as they listened through
their earphones, ringed
around the crystal set.

No need for electricity;
they had the whisker radio
ninety years ago –
and the family planned
their seaside holiday
with maps to tell them
where the best reception was.

Resorts of Blackpool, Cromer
and Llandudno could all receive
the time-check pips

Blank Canvas

beamed out from Daventry;
and now, generations on,
the good old BBC
still transmits to me – digitally.

SUNDAYS

When Clint was Rowdy
on black-'n'-white TV,
and Dad laughed staccato
at quick-fire Sgt Bilko
on dull Sunday afternoons
and wallowed with Hancock
on the wireless set;

And when ice cream
chimes stood in for cinema
silhouette of usher
popcorn girl who weekday
evenings showed us
to our seats by torchlight –

I preferred to be outside
catching grasshoppers
and wondering at the way
they leaped and how
their colour varied
to match the fields of weeds;

And now they're gone,
tarmacked by earthbound
crunch and press of time;

Blank Canvas

but you can still see repeats of old TV
or resurrect the mournful
mirth of Tony Hancock
on hissing steam-sound radio.

WALKING ON THE WIND

With rasping sighs
the breeze-brashed branches
fling their russetness
through churning skies
to crust the ground
with autumn's pall –
a detritus to delight us
in the coughed-out calm
that follows squall;
and then, oh glory be,
the warmth of sunshine
roding through
the now-still stands
of starkled trees –
as, fussed by feet,
the crispiness of leaves
fumes breathed-in air
with bitter nuttiness!

BLANK CANVAS

The hardest thing, I always think,
is making that first move –
seizing the moment of the mood,
for blank stands the canvas,
yearning for the beat of colour,
that signal of intent.

Imagine you're behind a microphone
and must sing that opening phrase
unrehearsed, or slide
into the trombone blow;
but then you know
it can only be in blue.

So you stand at the crossroads,
palette winking paint
– every wodge represents a GO;
now dare you be a Daniel?
Go on, improvise, extemporise
– oh, just get on with it,
aim the gun and SHOOT.

With that first precision dab
you make your mark, select
your ground – all things
stem from that one shape;
now, burdened with destiny,
that little dot of paint

Turn Now the Tide

is a challenge to the pristine
whiteness, urging its response.

But this attack is just too
tentative, too subdued...
and then you see, in your
mind's eye, how other artists
painted with such relish;
how then to emulate the lunge
and plunge of Pollock?
Or slash and parry of other
paintbrush swordsmen?

No. Re-begin with swash and buckle gusto,
shouting now: Take that, you snivelling
canvas. Splash into the turpentine,
wallop into the globs of paint,
frantic flourish on the palette
and then fierce stabs of colour
on the wretched, cowering surface.

The spell is broken,
sickly inhibitions roll away;
you grab the biggest brush
and fall upon the easel
with a blind and berserk fury.

Breathless, you stop to view
the carnival of carnage,
to inspect your desecration;
but now a new, more subtle
force has come upon you:

Blank Canvas

This won't do, you say.
Change gear. Select another mood,

More serene. Call it indigo.
Picasso would have approved!
So you slop and prod with bristle brush
and shapes take form –
like burnt sienna blushings
you may see in the fresh-cut
section of a tree.

Then your mind begins to wander,
straying into strange places – like:

> *Why do women hug cushions?*
> *I tried once and felt a fool,*
> *so I placed it behind*
> *my head and slept instead.*

Now, the moving, moody brush
has fashioned you a smiling face,
a young girl, you think
– your Mona Lisa, who just knows
that bilateral symmetry is SO BORING!

Turn Now the Tide

TURNED ON

Twice each year when seasons
changed and clocks went to and fro,
the lamp man cycled down our street
and tilted at the lines of lights
with his long hooked time-switch stick.

We always heard him come –
for as well as his switching lance
he carried a breezy song:
'The naughty lady of Shady Lane
had the town in a whirl...'
but the words 'come-hither glances'
were lost on the mind of a child.

Overcome with curiosity, I climbed
the fence one day and leaned across
to open up the lamp-post box and heard
it tick inside; reaching out to change
the hour (for a bit of devilment),
I felt an eel run up my arm –
which gave me quite a shock.

So turned on, I was, that I tried
it out at home – unscrewing
switches of brown Bakelite
and poking fingers in: blow me
if I didn't get a buzz from that.

Soon we two brothers competed

Blank Canvas

for a dare, counting as we did
to win a shock endurance game;
the lights went off when I got to six
– and Mum called out the ambulance.

We never chanced it after that,
but still today the current flows
and sparks my life electrically.
Now the only tingling that I get
is from a shady lady's smile
– a come-hither glance
to light the world and me.

BUDDING SCHOPENHAUER

The world
was my
idea,
the amoeba
said, dividing
and
multiplying
with no
ethical
sense
at all.

TIGER ON THE DOORSTEP

Tiger on the Doorstep

SHADES OF YOU

At night when you're away from me
I start to paint your memory:
how you seemed to me, in pastel
shades, last day we met.

Sometimes, acrylic's best
– or stark black lines of ink
to plot the jagged mood I'm in.

You see, when I paint or draw,
we're all the one,
a passion marled and intricate,
born on my palette.

And if my sable brush should dally
on your face – or other regions
of your naked form – I feel
your presence too,
for that's the art of love.

OFF BEAT

You play it, you play it
like this
'cause it's the wrong note song

You write it, you write it
like this
'cause it's the wrong word rhyme

You do it, you do it
like this
'cause it's the wrong way line

But set it to time
and the rhythm's sublime

NEVER ASK

I tell myself: Never
ask an actor
what he's at;
never ask a writer
what's the plot –
'specially if she knows
you also write;
never ask a poet
what he's rhyming,
or an artist
what she plans to paint
– they'll never tell the truth.
And so we sit together,
my friends and I,
and contemplate our silence,
not daring take
that extra drink
which might give
sudden way to our
ego-anchored tongues.

Turn Now the Tide

THE ICENI WAY, 1955

In line abreast they come –
yellow dozers licensed to destroy,
pulverising history into rubble;
demise of a stately Tudor home
on whose creaking, polished floors
we two brothers had once played.

But now that imperious advance
claws out the bricks and clay
and uproots noble oaken stumps
to scoop and ladle man-made
dross into the ancient,
living-breeding stretch of pond.

And, on the other side, scores
of frightened warty, hump-backed
orange-bellied newts – the rarest
kind – scramble up the bank
to flee their shrinking home.

There we meet them, we young
boys, conservationists of another
age, and scoop the fleeing evets
into buckets, bowls and jam-jars,
then cycle off to safer habitats
– out of bureaucratic reach
of the compulsory purchase men.

That Sunday next, a gang of angry

Tiger on the Doorstep

nature-loving boys and girls
descend – oh so stealthily –
on that deserted building site
to lay it waste in a Baudicean
orgy of great crested newt revenge.

Turn Now the Tide

COME BACK, CATULLUS

So, Catullus, you wrote
a lot of near-the-knuckle
stuff, couched in rhythms
that defied analysis
– chasing your Lesbia
with the urgent relish
of iambic and trochaic time.

Sex to you was the measure
of your effervescent age,
all of two thousand years ago;
that will to shock
still seems so relevant,
as does your odyssey
through the grossness
of Roman high society
– whilst civil wars
and caesars seized the day.

Now it is we who endure
such tribulation,
with equal need
for desperate diversion;
so, Catullus, grab us
by the short 'n' curlies,

Tiger on the Doorstep

tell us how to conjugate
the truth – as patrician
politicians defaecate
their circuses of lies.

Turn Now the Tide

DOWN BASIN STREET

Oh love, as long
as you can love,
come and go with me
down Basin Street,
where you'll meet
Liszt's *Liebestraum*
in another beat –
down the Mississippi
to the land of our dreams,
ferried on the trumpet
of saint Louis'
blue nocturne.

And so collective memory
of music paints
a sequence of the chords
on the mizzen of our mind;
Armstrong's version
of the song reflects
a beauty classically
contrived and sparked
by words about mankind's
enduring love; and soon
the hour will come
when old friends speak
again – down Basin Street,
the place where we all meet.

Tiger on the Doorstep

In tribute to composer Franz Liszt (1811–86), poet Ferdinand Freiligrath (1810–76), jazzman Louis Armstrong (1901–71).

This poem references the long sequences of chords in Basin Street Blues *and their similarity to a section of Liszt's* Liebestraum; *also Freiligrath's poem 'O lieb, so lang du lieben kannst' – on which Liszt's work is based – is echoed in the message of* Basin Street *and the meeting again of friends in an afterlife. Coincidence, or what?*

Turn Now the Tide

RUBBLER RHYS

Into the house
the hardy man came
from the field;
no word was said
as he stomped
his mud boots
on the slate-slatted floor,
while his wife
fussed over his tea.

No word was said
as he tore at the bread
with his split spaded nails,
clay-grouted
from scrawping potatoes
all rain-sodden day.

No word was said,
not even a sound,
as she watched her man eat,
her thoughts not of pity –
or even disgust,
but of pride and of dread
for his new job next week
was under the ground.

No word was said
but she knew that

Tiger on the Doorstep

each day she'd pray
for her mining man's
safe return.

Then, as he supped
at his tea,
their eyes challenged
and held in a love
that would meld
them as one.

'Don't worry, my dove,
I'll always be coming
back home to thee.'

***

Three wavering notes
the bugler blew
and the quarrymen
ran from the cave;
the clogwyn walls
repeated the sound
with the surge
of an echoing wave;
and then a great hush
as the rockmen
readied the charge.

The first blast came
with a rumbling thump
and a tumble of slate

Turn Now the Tide

as the heart of the mountain
broke with a quake.

When the dust cloud
rolled from the cavern's
wide maw, one fearful
shout was joined
by a roar:
'Where's Rhys?' they cried.
'We saw him before.'

His body was found,
crushed by the slate;
poor Rubbler Rhys
had been too deaf
to hear from time
at the Front
with world war
in his ear.

> *Gareth 'Rubbler' Rhys*
> *Blaenau Ffestiniog*
> *North Wales*
> *1894–1926*

SHADOWS ON A WALL

Now that I am alone again,
I yearn for days when fair
was fair and the russet
rustle of a ten-bob note
meant we had enough to share;

And when seasons came and went
unchanged by calamitous event;

And when my brother lay across
from me and fiddled with his torch
while we made shadows on the wall,
unafraid of Father who'd fought
a war that made him hurt us all;

And now at night I know my friends
are there for me, their faces caught
in that consoling beam of light.

Turn Now the Tide

GETTING ON

Will I be dragged
away one day
to join old ladies
playing Bezique
and drinking tea
with woollen rugs
across the knee?

Will I be wearing
cast-off clothes
too good to throw
away, yet fitting
now I've shrunk?

And will those
in charge address
me, patronisingly,
with the plural *we*?

How are we today?
they'll say
– and I will think:
Times were better
yesterday, you should
have known me then.

        Bitch!

HOT GOSSIP

June came in May;
you brought to me
this skimble-skamble
and scuttled off
with shielded grin.

That cleft-stick message
was your savoured
joke for the day,
but what you didn't know
– June was here
in April too. And July;
my friend, you were
too old to spy,
but I miss your company.

WHISPERER

Ears dipped forward,
heads lowered to her face,
they revel in the voice;
soft, caressing, teasing
and cajoling, sharing
sounds of solace;
they understand – it is
a mingling of the soul.

She speaks to them in Welsh
– whispers of the mountain
wind, of laughter borne
on water as it ripples
over rock; the horses
understand – and breathe
with the same inward breath;
they are as one.

Tiger on the Doorstep

HIRAETH

Although we never loved,
you gave me strength
when I was lost
and showed me other ways
to live alone once more.

I came to you at Croesor
and found a welcome
only Wales can give
– drawn back by rock
and stream and memory
of glowing mountain light.

Born on Moel-y-Gest,
I longed to see once more
that rugged, sharp profile
of dark Cnicht and climb
the path to Tryfan
or cross Crib Goch in snow
and row the Menai Strait
then feel the wash of rain,
knowing that the sun
would shine on me again.

Hiraeth: a yearning for one's place of being.

Turn Now the Tide

CURTAIN CALL

From apron platform range
he opened up
and sprayed the audience
with calligraphic singing voice
– words precisely formed
with scalloped vowels
and cleated consonants.

Legs firmly planted
on the stage,
he took his bow
and modestly absorbed
our 'Bravo' cries.

Next day we saw him
gliding down Main Street,
caped and wide-brim-hatted,
hands cupped to receive
the adulation of his fans.

Beyond the rest of us,
his art, his voice, his grace.
Basil Lovage, the programme
said, baritone on loan
from the world's great stage.

WATCHERS

Mizzen tail held high, the distant
watcher side-stepped on the branch,
prating all the while, drawing
other magpies to its grandstand view.

Soon there were two – but not for joy
with what they had in mind;
sorrow beckoned to the object
of their gorgon gaze.

For on the broken bridge below,
another bird of black and white
flitted through the morning mist,
bearing shags of moss
to chosen nesting site.

The shapely little dipper,
that curtsied constantly,
would never live to see
the hatching of her eggs.

CAVE PAINTINGS

In vans and trucks marked
CHOCOLATE, the old masters
came in convoy – Wales
their destination from galleries
of blitz-hit London town.

Churchill's orders said
they must be safely stored
in caverns deep beneath
a mountain, away from Hitler's
undiscerning bombs.

Slate mines of Blaenau
became their hiding place,
Blake's mad King of Babylonia
alongside Van Dyck's Charles I,
on horseback underground.

Now they're all back home
again, hanging in the light
at the National and the Tate,
dusted down and shining
– until the next time round.

RHYTHM OF A DIVE

Check the pressure,
check the depth,
time is creeping on;
switch off the torch.
Concentrate.

Finning slowly through the forest,
fronds of fucus waving by;
follow weaving conger
to its clefted hideaway.
Keep well clear.

Now it watches
from the blackness.
Paranoia.

Time to end the dive;
follow bubbles upwards
to the light.
Stay alive.

Turn Now the Tide

COLD WAR GRAN

The day that Gran changed sides
took us all completely by surprise:
listening at the wall,
tapping messages with her walking stick,
talking to the Russians;
her Cold War madness,
brought on by a tiny stroke,
made her, briefly, a double agent;
but a bit of basket work
in the local shrink resort
cured her of all that non-sense
and she became a citizen again,
saner than the rest of us;
the Russians had retreated
from our Welsh hillside home,
but elsewhere the spies spied on.

IN THE BIBLICAL SENSE

Alone in a hotel room,
I turned to Gideon
and read myself to sleep,
but disquiet came in dreams
of threesome romps
with Ruth and Jezebel –
and when I cried out 'Rachel!'
all hell broke loose...

Turn Now the Tide

PARROT VOTE

On the stump I was,
touting for their Number One
– candidate of independent
air, who dreamed of fixing life
for people left behind.

Vote for Me was this man's mantra
as he knocked and waited
at the umpteenth door;
no response, so to the back instead
– and there it was,
blue parrot in a cage,
drowsing in the midday sun.

What politician would miss
that opportunity?
I'll teach it to speak my name
for all to hear;
Vote Neal, I said to it, repeatedly,
forgetting that Neal sounds like No
to an Irish-speaking bird.

And then, eventually, sitting
by the cage – shirt and feathers
blue on blue – I fell asleep,
to be wakened by a raucous
crooning from the perch
above my head:

Tiger on the Doorstep

Vote Neal – Vote Neal – Vote Neal.
Who said democracy was dead?
Endorsement from a parrot
was no Monty Python joke...

PIKE

Just look at him:
those flanks of willow green
stencilled by the sun,
forward mien of mouth
that harbours so much grudge;
you've got to sock it to him,
old Esox, reaper of the river,
he's the villain you just love to hate.

How we anglers flatter him
with spinner, fly and plug
–and even living bait,
but he taunts us all
by moving in on worm
or crusty bread
intended for more dainty
pluckers of the hook.

PATHFINDER

Your moon-path home shines
through the mossy *migneint*
– bogland safely marked
in times long gone
by hardy men with hefty
stones of quartz –
but beware the glower
of glow-worms,
showing out on scattered
heather clumps;
they are the wreckers'
lamps luring you astray.

NOT QUITE LEGLESS

He lay in bed,
carving chess pieces
from the wood
of his false leg.

He knew he'd never
have the strength
to walk again;
life from then would
be a different game
– more skilled,
and thus fulfilled.

Tiger on the Doorstep

YE SHALL NOT LAUGH

Why is there no humour
in the Bible – is the joke
a cosmic one?
I asked a rabbi once;
Look at the Book of Amos,
you'll find it there, he said.

Seven times I read the script
and still could not divine
the fun – not without HIS faith;
though by all accounts,
in Sodom and Gomorrah
THEY knew how to laugh.

Turn Now the Tide

EVER AND EVER

Feel the camel's pitching roll,
articulate the yaw,
lean into the hump, stare before,
fix the eye on the next dune ridge:
horizon's where it meets the sky.

Feel the wind-blown rhythm of the sands,
grasp that green's a colour you can only think
– that running water's but a dream;
count the desert particles
to keep the mind in sync.

There has to be an end
to all of this, just has to be…

TIGER ON THE DOORSTEP

Being with you was such ecstasy,
as if all tenses had become
the one – passions pulling
silken threads of past,
present and of future
into a triptych of ourselves.

But then a blackened quirk
of chance carried you away
and I was left bereft
of that better part of me,

Until the night I saw,
lighting up my doorstep,
the incandescent colours
of a garden tiger moth –
reminder that your beauty
had never left this earth.

Turn Now the Tide

ANOTHER BRIDGET

I knew a Bridget once;
she wore a cape each day
to hospital where her
sick patients lay.

At night she spread
it on her bed
and led young men astray;
doctors, students
– they all came
to her to be shown
the way to love.

Afterwards she used
that cape to shield
her child from life's mistake.
But, precious as he was
to her, she lost
her little joy.

His life was not to be
– and like a dainty
hatching mayfly,
lasted but a day.

Instead of tearing up
her life with tears,
this Bridget returned
to the island

Tiger on the Doorstep

of her birth and spread
again her cape
over those whose lives,
through illness,
had been ordained
a determined end,
and in hospice found
the love and care
of Bridget – saint.

ODD IZZIE, 2001

It was as if old Mogue
had dined on magic
mushrooms;
his usual forensic
stutterings,
his castles of bricked-up
syllogisms,
seemed to lack
the premises of probability.

He was telling us
what his friend Izzie
had said,
just before he died:
'Will I dream, Mogue,
when I am
deactivated?'

SKYFALL

Anticipating
Ronan's curse,
Sweeney climbs
the tree
– but fails
to see
a woodman
sharpening
his axe.

No way will
he escape
his destiny.

RIVER SONG

River Song

MUSIC OF ANTRIM

Bring her the harps
and hammer dulcimers
of dreaming County Antrim;
let music be the swirl
of mist enfolding
memory with time.

Still, from a continent away,
she sees blue-knuckled hills
cuffed by lush of trees –
and puffs of dirty gunsmoke cloud
curling in the breeze.

But for those plucked
sounds, she would be blind.

GET OUT OF MY GARDEN

Like High Noon cowboys
squaring up to death,
two cock robins sing
their fearsome song –
to terrorise for territory.

Only one can win his choice
– the other banished
from the garden
by his discordant voice.

River Song

SKY WALKER

I found you as the sun came up,
walking with your wings
and tumbling down each step
as you teetered on the edge,
and when I took you in my hand
you clicked your tongue
and trembled with the rhythm
of a tiny beating heart.

Drops of sugared water helped,
I think, before I brought you up
a ladder to the hole your parents
used as access to their rooftop home;
I hope they didn't give your lugs
a tweak for doing a runner down
the stairs while they slept on,
you little long-eared bat.

Turn Now the Tide

INTO THE GULLEY

Led on by screaming officer
with stick and pistol gun,
we did the chicken run –
knowing bullets couldn't
carry *all* the names we had.

Pals beside me paid the debt
but I charged on, drawn
by thrust of my own bayonet
– and I was through.

Shrapnel Gulley, they called
the valley – Snipers' Alley,
I'd have said!
We were the ANZACs
– 9th Battalion, A Company,
to be precise; sergeant me,
from Wales – not an Oz.

I just went there for a job
– but this war came up
and I volunteered to do my bit;
wearing glasses made no differ,
they said to me, you'll carry
a rifle, cobber, like the rest of 'em.

Gallipoli's an awful place,
the Dardanelles all the hells
in one; I was seasick

River Song

when we landed, so much noise
from whiz-bang shells and gun.

No time to think, just move on;
kill the Turks or they'll kill you.
Whose king? Whose country?
I don't know. Are you safe at home?
Are the Turks in Sydney yet?
Or up my North Wales mountain
– chasing sheep?

The telegram you're reading
now says *Missing Believed Dead*.
No one knows where I rest my head.
Just another body in the Gulley;
the war that didn't end all wars.
Think of me when you buy that poppy
– it's the colour of our blood.

> *James Muncaster Lovett, 303, Sgt. Infantry. 9th Battalion, South Australian Regiment. Missing believed killed. Last seen escorting prisoners, Shrapnel Gulley, Dardanelles, April 25th 1915. Gallipoli Peninsula. Slaughter of the Innocents. RIP.*

Turn Now the Tide

EAR TRUMPET

When their neighbours
complained of the noise,
my old uncle and aunt
were forced to move out
– but they found a new home
by the sea, where deafening
waves bore their shouted
sweet-nothings away;
I still have the trumpet,
with handle and all,
which blew their
affectionate yells;
Percy and Jess, your lives
were a fanfare of love.

River Song

TOO WET TO WOO

We shared a great hope
when we met in the rain,
two people who talked
of things that went wrong
in the beautiful game;

One brolly she had
to fend off the shower,
but when the wind tugged
and cast it afar
we parted and ran,
wet strangers again.

HIS FAIRY QUEENE

The passion flowers
beside the bed
failed to make complete
the night she couldn't sleep
for fear she wouldn't wake
from pills that beat the pain.

But still they had each other
for that longest year together
– long enough to know how wrong
the poet's rhyme that death 'does
greatly please' as we pick our way
through lichen-measured time.

ALPHA AND OMEGA

Your unctuous cat
declares its presence
Greekly, referencing
the coefficient of viscosity,
then slimes away lubriciously
– all green platonic stare –
and leaves behind its sticky
plaything, still warm
yet bereft of any destiny.

FOXGLOVE FISH

Digitalis purpurea,
your litmus-red
appearance is the acid
test which marks
the first sea trout
run, fox glove sentinel
whose bugle call of colour
summons up the fish.

River Song

TURN NOW THE TIDE

Welcome back the springs
of returning tide,
of life once more shared
with someone else;
waves of such gentle clash
that meet and mingle,
fondly coalesce –
bringing brightness
where once sadness
sucked out all the light.

Drench me with the honey
of your soothing voice,
lift my soul so high
it joins you in
that self-same song
– duet of swelling happiness,
riding on the surf of love.

Turn Now the Tide

CATCHER IN THE SKY

Word is, brother, you've moved on
– gone to another place,
left no forwarding address,
but I know otherwise: you see,
you're still with me in my mind;
I just have to close my eyes.

Others say they saw you
looking peaceful
after all those tests,
and later you were carried
off, quite ornately,
as the compliments
kept coming – like cake
to a cricket commentary box.

But you're there,
out in the field
at deep backward square
leg, waiting for the catch.

River Song

RIDING HIGH

You could tell the land
had once been flooded
for there were horses
in the trees;

Now just skeletons,
they hang askew
– unstrapped saddles
on the bare-back branches,
reminder that in death
there is no nobility.

Turn Now the Tide

TUMBLING DOWN

Through the skylight
I see sheep staring
down at me when I awake;
really, it's no joke –
for my cottage
hangs along a slope.

Springtime's best when acrobatic
lambs flounce around the roof
and daffodils stand in
for the yellow of the morning sun.

But now the farmer's
sold his flock and grows
the grass to make
gigantic bales
of winter fodder feed.

So steep the slope,
the ricks of Weetabix
roll off and tumble past
the roof while I'm asleep.

Will my nightmare
obit say he died
in bed, crushed
by a ton of hay?

Or that the ceiling broke

River Song

and he and silage plunged
to the kitchen range below
to be consumed, Viking-style,
in a blazing funeral pyre?

Oh, please, let no more be said!

Turn Now the Tide

VINEGAR HILL

When the peregrine stoops
on Vinegar Hill
the People will rise
to be free.

So the soothsayers said,

But they failed to tell
of the blood that would spill
over bright summer rock
as whole families fought
with their hands
to be equal
to all other Men.

You may see that falcon today
as it sweeps the red sky
with wings that spread hope
to a world that still strives
to be free.

But best you beware,

For when the peregrine stoops
on Vinegar Hill
the People may rise yet again.

River Song

To the brave people who died on Cnoc Fhiodh na gCaor (Vinegar Hill), Enniscorthy, Co. Wexford, Ireland, in 1798.

Turn Now the Tide

BEGGING NOW

Are you just my sometime
friend – one who switches
on and off like a storage
heater in the night?
Or do you really mean it
when you say you do?

Talk is cheap, action speaks
louder – and we get enough
of that each week we meet
– but I'm getting tired
of missing you when you're away,
living that other life.
I'm yours; be mine this time
– for all time... please?

Oh, all right, I'll try
another tack: you are the shadow
of a butterfly, pinned
to my mind by the noon-day sun;
or maybe: beauty shrinks the debit
side of youthfulness; yes, these are
my best chat-up lines, I'll admit,
but I really do mean what I say.

Please believe me – desperate now
– I'll take the test: a falling
blossom only touches lips

River Song

that lie (I'm safe here – spring
is still a whole winter away!).

Turn Now the Tide

MUSSEL MAN

One hundred and thirty
seven mussels lay
opened at his feet,
dredged up that day
from the fringes
of Loch Neagh
– and not a pearl
in one; dead
swan mussels
– but, living
still, his greed.

River Song

DUCK CALL

So no more to be heard,
the sucked-in whistle
of this wild teal bird,
felled from sky by scattered
shot above wetland slob
and gathered up in gentle
jaws of black retriever dog.

So no more down of wispy,
chestnut brown; this silenced
duck lies naked pink,
plucked and stuffed with apricot
– all ready for the pot;
casseroled to be consumed
by wingless, grounded, civil man.

Turn Now the Tide

SINGLE-HANDED

One arm hung loose as he walked,
fingers stretched to grasp another;
it was the way he always went
– relentless trudge of a man
whose life was once complete.

> *But birds still sing*
> *and quicksands shift*
> *to hide the moment's print.*

How she'd clung to him as hip to hip
they'd strode, unaware of jealous
time's calamitous approach.

> *But birds still sing*
> *and quicksands shift*
> *to hide the moment's print.*

And now he tilts his head and smiles
towards the empty, dangling hand.

> *For birds still sing*
> *and quicksands shift*
> *to hide the moment's print.*

River Song

MISTER SOFTEE

The chimes of Mister Softee
blend in so well
with tolls of morning Mass,
but ice cream marks
the wafer-thin division
of this community.

ARMED GRAFFITI BADGES WALLS
BESIDE THE ROAD THAT FALLS
ALONG THE LINE THAT TELLS
US WHO WE THINK WE ARE

So let's all queue
together and buy a cornet
and make believe
we live in peace.

Written after a visit to Belfast in the sad old days

Turn Now the Tide

RIVER SONG

Listen, it's night-time by the river
when sights all come as sound –
those scuffles, rustles, swishes, snaps
– as otter, fox and badger,
stoat and bankside vole, go about their round;

And when the shoving sea raises streaming
water high and tames its gurgling purl
into a smooth and gentle whirl,
and when its skin is broken only
by sipping trout sucking down a fly;

But soon, with dawn, the time will come
when tide begins to draw away and the swoosh
and gush of unimpeded downstream
flow will bring again the music
that I have learned to see and know.

River Song

CASTING

I love the swish and wish
of casting for a fish:
up-two-three; down-two-three
– like giving a salute,
the 'officer' a trout
you're wanting to impress.

Ratchet on the reel,
corncrakes in the field
become a buzzing bee
when brownie's hooked
through rod and line to me.

LEARNING CURVE

The sparrow hawk, fierce
of orange eye, barred
feathers rufous, blue and white,
stood sedate, centre stage,
on a branch above the barn.

Beside her dithered
two young ones, stage right;
below, as 'twere on apron front,
a rabbit munched and sniffed
and hopped a bit
– but never once looked up.

The scene was set, missing,
though, the buskined hero
belting out his tragic monologue.

Now watch on.

With sideways sliding glide,
the hook-beaked mother hawk
hangs above the furry innocent,
yellow legs and claws thrust out
– and shows the way to pounce.

Children follow suit, clumsily,
and then back off, mewing
like the cats they definitely are not.
Three times they perform this act
and then fly off together,

River Song

hunting lesson dusted, done.

Exit rabbit, stage left,
not even chased.
Life's a game. This time…

LOVE'S VELOCITY

It was not just the look
of you that did for me;
not your eyes,
your voice alone
– it was your presence.

It took a millisecond
for me to know I was in love.
Of course, I doubted
my own sanity;
pragmatism said:
Get a grip on reality.

But afterwards you told me
you were smitten too
– and then I woke,
I knew it wasn't true.

River Song

GUARDIANS OF TIME

I saw the wild geese standing
in a hilly, stubbled field
where once a church had been;

So still they were, like tilting
silhouettes of broken stone,
spaced apart and facing to the east;

Guardians of memory in a cemetery of old
– people long, long gone, their lives
but a jiffy in the universe of time;

Then suddenly the birds just upped
and flapped away in staggered line
across the pleated moonlit sky;

It was as if they'd never been,
the church and graveyard
just a note in books of history.

Turn Now the Tide

PRICKLE

Oh, why did I ever start
to count your freckles?
It's not because you have
so many; it was just my way
of testing boundaries,
having a bit of fun
at your expense – as you're
always doing to me.

How was I to know
that you'd declare
a war of independence?
Wave the flag
of Spots and Stripes?
Want to rule the world?

What was I to do but make
myself a controlling state
as well – the Hammer
and Sickle one?
Our Cold War has just begun.

Which one of us is going
to join the CND?
Give up the deterrent
and make peace again?
It won't be me!

River Song

WHAT SHALL IT BE?

Jock Scott looks good;
I like the colour.
I'll try this one
and tie it to the line;
no, hold on, Thunder
and Lightning might
be more the thing.

The names are what
pull me in;
now a Hairy Mary
might just do it
– or maybe a Silver
Doctor will cure
my indecision.

I shall be all day
on the river bank,
so perhaps I'll change
the fly each cast
– until the salmon
gets as hooked as me.

DAY OF THE DINOSAUR

Is there a fine place
outside our own world
where people can grow
from their mortal mistakes?

Aristophanes held so
two millennia ago
– though his fanciful
Birds and his Wasps
and his Frogs made
comical conflict seem
more than the norm.

But the Chorus still asks
if ever we'll learn.

Better the dinosaurs
had stayed to save Earth
– though terror of kings
is a gene that lives on.

River Song

UNDERSTANDING GODOT

If you conate,
like Lucky on a rope,
and relate
a camogie glide
or skate
stark-naked
in the stockinged feet,
you'll cognate,
affectively,
and find the key
to Godot
without a pause too long.

Still confused?
There's no Endgame here;
you have to DO the play
the Beckett way.

www.ingramcontent.com/pod-product-compliance
Lightning Source LLC
Chambersburg PA
CBHW022119040426
42450CB00006B/768